Organ Preludes on Favorite Hymns

Arranged by JOYCE JONES

Joyce Jones

When Joyce Jones plays one of her famous pedal solo encores she often tells her audience that it is her way of saying "Thank You" to God for showing her the direction for her life. While a piano student in her native Texas, she suffered a badly sprained hand, and it seemed her life's dream of becoming a concert pianist was shattered. However, she began to practice pedals on the organ and discovered a natural flair and coordination for that instrument. What seemed to be a tragedy turned out to be a most fortunate accident, from which developed one of the greatest organists of our time.

Joyce Jones seemed destined for a future in music since her childhood. She began piano lessons at the age of four and composed music at the age of six. She graduated from the University of Texas with highest honors at the age of nineteen, and began teaching there on a fellowship. Nine months later she earned her first of two master's degrees. Joyce Jones also holds a Doctor of Musical Arts degree in organ performance. She is currently head of the organ department and Organist in residence at Baylor University, the world's largest Baptist university.

Dr. Jones had her debut as soloist with the Dallas Symphony Orchestra and has gone on to perform concerts throughout the United States, Canada, Mexico, Central America, Japan and Europe. She has performed in such noted halls at the Mormon Tabernacle and Notre Dame Cathedral, and was the first woman to play the famed organ at the Crystal Cathedral. She was also the only woman organist selected to play on the gala concert inaugurating the new Ruffatti organ at Davies Symphony Hall in San Francisco.

As one of the first artists to take classical organ music to small communities, Joyce Jones continues to make new friends for the concert organ. She constantly receives rave reviews for her dazzling, virtuosic technique, which combined with personal warmth leaves audiences thrilled. Joyce Jones is known as the organist other organists come to hear.

Contents

The Church's One Foundation / **8**

Come, Ye Sinners / **24**

Glorious Things of Thee are Spoken / **54**

Holy, Holy, Holy / **28**

I Love Thee / **12**

Jesus, Lover of My Soul / **38**

Jesus Shall Reign Where 'er the Sun / **22**

My Hope is Built on Christ, the Solid Rock / **4**

My Jesus, I Love Thee / **49**

Rejoice, the Lord is King / **52**

Rescue the Perishing / **44**

Sweet Hour of Prayer / **19**

We're Marching to Zion / **42**

What a Friend We Have In Jesus / **16**

To Nita and Jake Akin

MY HOPE IS BUILT ON CHRIST, THE SOLID ROCK

(The Solid Rock)

SW: Trumpet 8'
GT: Foundations 8', 4'
PED: Foundations 16', 8', Gt. to Ped.

Arranged by Joyce Jones

To Father Ted Nelson and
the Episcopal Church of the Resurrection, Dallas, Texas

THE CHURCH'S ONE FOUNDATION
(Aurelia)

SW: Flute 8'
GT: Chimes
CH: Harp (or Flutes 8', 2')
PED: Soft 16', 8'

Arranged by Joyce Jones

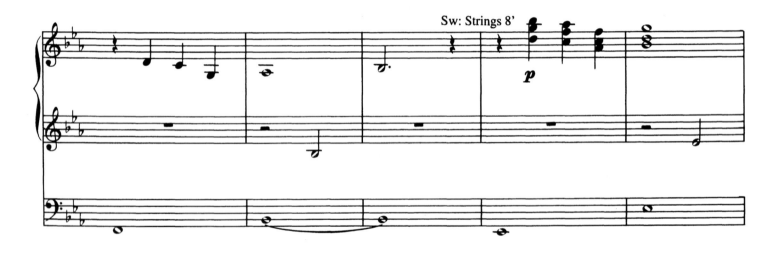

To Emelie and Walter Spivey

I LOVE THEE

(I Love Thee)

SW: Solo Stop 8'
GT: Flutes 8', 4'
PED: Soft 16', 8'

Arranged by Joyce Jones

To Dr. Laney Johnson and Mobberly Avenue Baptist Church

WHAT A FRIEND WE HAVE IN JESUS
(Converse)

SW: Flutes 8', 4'
GT: Flutes 8', 2 2/3', 1 3/5'
PED: Bourdons 16', 8'

Arranged by Joyce Jones

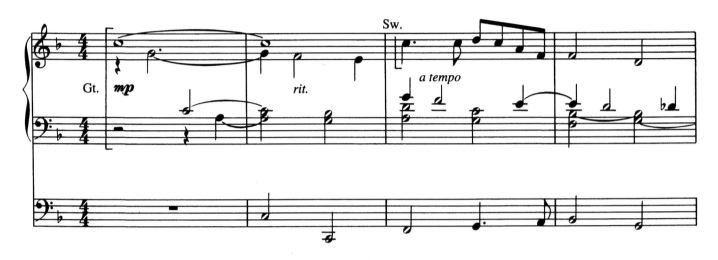

To Lucile and Earl Miller

SWEET HOUR OF PRAYER
(Sweet Hour)

SW: Strings 8'
GT: Flute 8'
PED: Soft 16', 8'

Arranged by Joyce Jones

To Linda and David Pennington

JESUS SHALL REIGN WHERE'ER THE SUN
(Trio on "Duke Street")

SW: Flutes 8', 2'
GT: Principal 8', (or Flutes 8', 4')
PED: Bourdons 16', 4'

Arranged by Joyce Jones

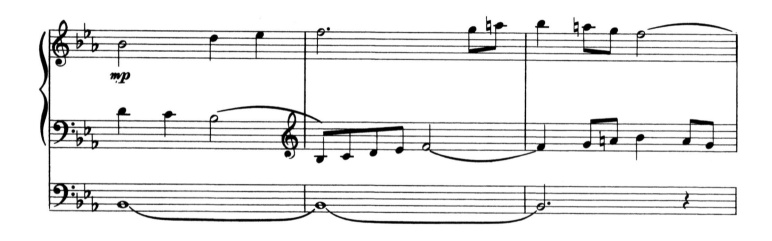

poco rit.

To Elenor and William McClure

COME, YE SINNERS
(Restoration)

SW: Strings 8'
GT: Flutes 8', 2 2/3'
PED: Bourdons 16', 8'

Arranged by Joyce Jones

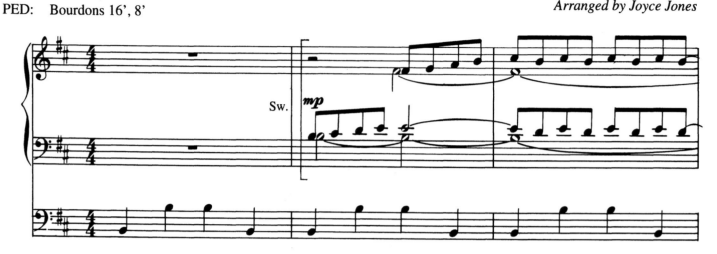

May also be played with accompaniment on Great: Flute 8' and melody on Swell: Flute 8' and 2¾',
changing to Oboe for left hand.

To Elinor and William Doty

HOLY, HOLY, HOLY
(Introduction, Air and Toccata on "Nicaea")

SW: Strings 8'
GT: Soft Flute 8', Sw. & Ch. to Gt.
CH: Flute 8', Flute Celeste 8'
PED: Soft 16', (32'), Sw. to Ped.

Arranged by Joyce Jones

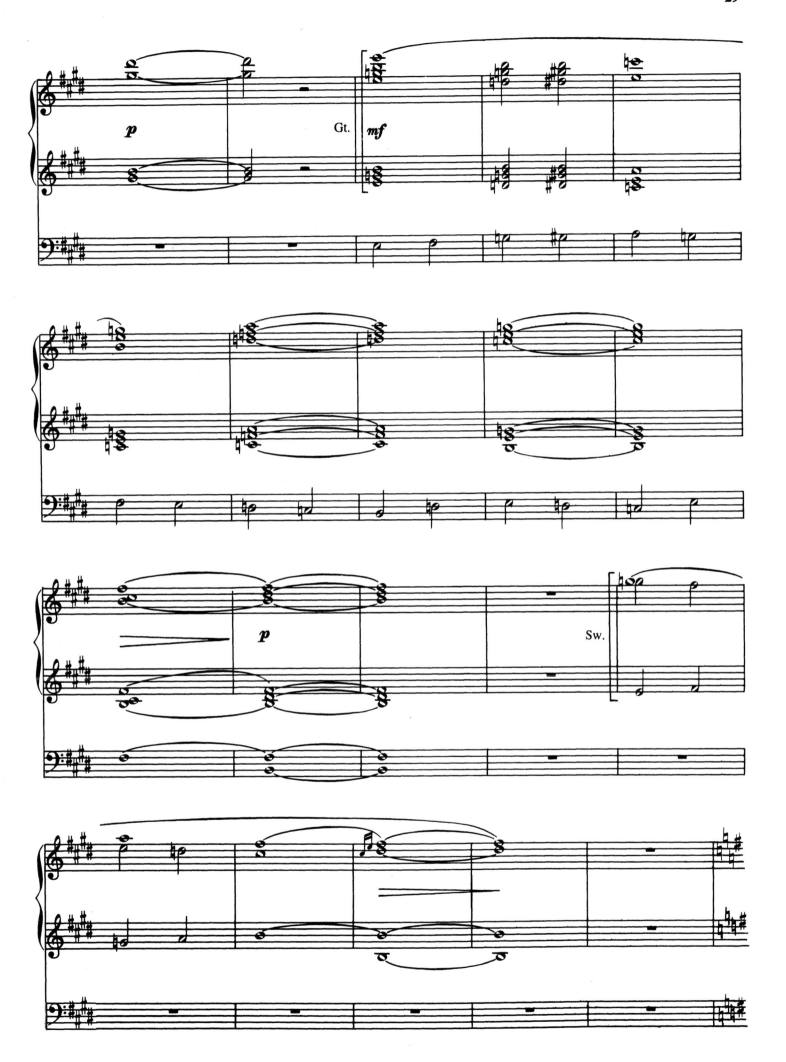

off Sw. to Ped.

Sw.

Ch.

prepare Sw. Fl. 8', 2'

p

To Marjorie and Gordon Psalmonds

JESUS, LOVER OF MY SOUL
(Aberystwyth)

SW: Oboe 8' Flute 4'
GT: Flute 8'
PED: Soft 16', 8'

Arranged by Joyce Jones

To the Fred Mitchell family and First Baptist Church of Mexia, Texas

WE'RE MARCHING TO ZION
(Marching to Zion)

SW: Flutes 8', 2' (1 1/3')
GT: Soft Solo Reed 8'
PED: 16', 4'

Arranged by Joyce Jones

To Doyce Deas and Harrisburg Baptist Church, Tupelo, Mississippi

RESCUE THE PERISHING
(Rescue)

SW: Flutes 8', 2'
GT: Flutes 8', 4', 2', (1 1/3'
PED: Flutes 16', 4'

Arranged by Joyce Jones

Gt.

48

To Harold Gage

MY JESUS, I LOVE THEE
(Gordon)

SW: Flutes and Strings 8', 4'
GT: Solo Combination 8'
PED: 16', 8', Sw. to Ped.

Arranged by Joyce Jones

To Ann and Robert Flood

REJOICE, THE LORD IS KING
(Darwall's 148th)

SW: Principals and Flutes 8', 4', 2', Mixture
GT: Principals 8', 4', 2', Mixture, Reed 8'
PED: Principals 16', 8', 4', Sw. to Ped.

Arranged by Joyce Jones

To Josephine Canfield

GLORIOUS THINGS OF THEE ARE SPOKEN
(Austria)

SW: Trumpet 8'
GT: Foundations 8',4', 2'
PED: Foundations 16', 8', Gt. to Ped.

Arranged by Joyce Jones